Living with
Japanese Gardens

LIVING WITH
JAPANESE GARDENS

Chadine Flood Gong
and Lisa Parramore

Photography by Svein Olslund

Gibbs Smith, Publisher
Salt Lake City

WE DEDICATE THIS BOOK TO FRANK NUNEZ,
OUR PARTNER IN BUILDING JAPANESE GARDENS
FOR TWENTY-FIVE YEARS.

First Edition
10 09 08 07 06   5 4 3 2 1

Published 1-4236-0120-3 1-4236-0120-3 by
Gibbs Smith, Publisher
PO Box 667
Layton, Utah 84041

Orders: 1.800.748.5439
www.gibbs-smith.com

Design by Catherine Lau Hunt
Printed and bound in Hong Kong

Library of Congress Cataloging-in-Publication Data
Gong, Chadine Flood.
  Living with Japanese gardens / Chadine Flood Gong and Lisa Parramore ;
photography by Svein Olslund.—1st ed.
    p. cm.
  ISBN 1-58685-818-1
1. Gardens, Japanese. I. Parramore, Lisa. II. Title.

SB458.G665 2006
712.60952—dc22

2006007038

CONTENTS

ACKNOWLEDGMENTS

I would like to offer my heartfelt thanks to the homeowners who generously opened their homes and gardens to us.

I am indebted to the Fulbright Scholarship Program for providing me with the opportunity to come to the United States and then to Japan to live, study, and teach. I would also like to express particular gratitude to my late husband, Dr. E. Thadeus Flood, who was responsible for introducing me to a deeper understanding and appreciation of Japanese aesthetics and culture. Thanks also to my husband, Dr. Hayman Gong, for his unfailing encouragement, and, last but not least, to Frank Nunez for having constructed in the past twenty-five years more than one hundred Japanese gardens that I designed.

—Chadine Flood Gong

I would like to express my sincere gratitude to the homeowners who enthusiastically discussed their Japanese gardens with us. My thanks go also to the Japan Exchange and Teaching Program, which gave me the chance to live and work in Fukushima, Japan.

I would like to acknowledge Dr. Tracey Wilen-Daugenti, whose advice as a seasoned author helped get this project off the ground; to architect and author Sarah Susanka, who took the time to share her reactions to the book's photographs; to Dr. Kendall Brown, whose knowledge of the DeSabla Tea Garden was of great assistance; to Douglas Roth of the *Journal of Japanese Gardening* and fellow garden-designer Lynn Mitchell for their thoughtful comments and suggestions on the manuscript; and to Aimee Stoddard, our patient and thorough editor at Gibbs Smith, Publisher.

I would also like to thank my mother, Barbara Parramore; Rune Olslund and his family; and Miki Nagasaki on whose support I heavily relied. Finally, this book would not have been possible without my husband, Svein Olslund, whose prolific talents as a photographer and all-around technical guru never cease to amaze me.

—Lisa Parramore

INTRODUCTION

Upon learning of our passion for Japanese gardens, a dinner companion said, "If you spend any amount of time in Japan, you can't help but be infected by it." *It* in this case, is the Japanese aesthetic, reflected so elegantly in the country's art, architecture, and, of course, its gardens.

But even if you have never been to Japan, you can see the influence of Japanese gardens in many other places. There are several hundred public Japanese gardens in countries around the world. More and more, nurseries stock stone lanterns

A mature grove of bamboo provides an elegant welcome at Chadine Flood Gong's home.

The camellia tips
the remains of last
night's rain
splashing out.
—BUSON (1716–1784)

and water basins, elements intrinsic to many Japanese gardens. Koi enthusiasts have formed numerous clubs. Graceful culms of bamboo are shooting up, forming vertical screens in tight spaces or adding drama to roof-top gardens. The Internet makes ordering ornaments like rain chains easy, no matter where you live. And yet, the popularity of these elements alone does not explain the widespread interest in the Japanese garden. Rather, it is the ability of a Japanese garden to capture the essence of a landscape that affirms our connection with the natural world. It is the integration of the garden with the house that enriches the total living space. It is the artistry with which the gardener places plants, rocks, and water with the viewer's perspective in mind. In these ways, Japanese gardens have the ability to make us feel truly at home.

Japanese visitors to the United States often remark on how vast and open the landscape feels in contrast to their homeland, a relatively small, mountainous island country. The Japanese garden tradition evolved within these intimate confines, so perhaps it is no accident that Japanese gardens feel safe and sheltering. It is that sense of shelter combined with a well-developed aesthetic taste, which places great value on fine craftsmanship and the subtle beauty of asymmetry, that help explain the vast appeal of the Japanese garden in the West for well over a century. Indeed, one garden featured in this book, the De Sabla Japanese Tea Garden, has nurtured a succession of owners since it was first built circa 1906.

Residential gardens are restricted by size, shape, and topography of the land, the lifestyle of the homeowner, and, of course, by the budget. For the owner of a humble home on a modest lot, the Japanese garden is not only a superior form of landscape design but also a rejection of gaudiness. As Junichiro Tanizaki opined in his mid-twentieth-century volume of essays, *In Praise of Shadows*, "We [Japanese] find it hard to be really at home with things that shine and glitter."

A single camellia blossom, placed on a water basin, reminds one of early spring. This basin decorates a garden scene at the Ren Brown Gallery (see Special Moment, Special Place chapter).

Perhaps our similar discomfort with the shiny and new explains our renewed appreciation of rustic yet well-crafted items over the glossy and mass-produced objects of the Industrial Age. In his groundbreaking book, *Wabi-Sabi for Artists, Designers and Philosophers*, Leonard Koren introduced us to the Japanese sensitivity to things "imperfect, impermanent and incomplete." This intentional avoidance of perfection is realized in a number of garden features portrayed in this book: pine trees whose trunks are twisted and leaning, mossy paths in which unswept fallen petals are part of the charm, and even a bridge with missing planks that allows an unexpected glimpse of the water below.

The scarcity of land in many metropolitan areas leaves many homeowners with little outside space, but this is by no means an impediment to having a Japanese garden. Just as the "Not So Big House" movement advocates designing homes with a sense of shelter and comfort over pretentious "starter castles," this book shows you how a thoughtfully planned Japanese garden brings nature and art together to nurture the soul.

As our lives become filled with more and more high-tech devices and automated communication, we need accessible reminders of nature as a counterpoint to put the technological progress into perspective. Perhaps that endless voice mail menu will be more bearable if we can gaze onto what Tamao Goda described in the *Journal of Japanese Gardening* as "a landscape painting that we live inside of." Some of the gardens in this book, designed by the authors, are located in Silicon Valley, the fast-paced center of technological innovation. As Erica Schroeder said of the garden Lisa Parramore designed for the atrium of her home, "It's so entirely calming and centered—one almost forgets the frenetic Silicon Valley way of life." The same sentiments are expressed by Carol Swenson of the reflecting pool Chadine Flood Gong designed for her home: "In keeping with the Japanese tradition, Chadine is able to exercise a refined restraint in her designs. The result is an understated elegance that makes our garden interesting for us year after year."

The Japanese, intense participants in the technological age, nevertheless have held on to their distinctive view of nature. While famous historical gardens in Japan have the feel of museums crowded with tourists, and the average Japanese living space makes its Western counterpart seem palatial by comparison, there are special places where the tradition lives on. It could be a space as small as a restaurant entry that has a water basin surrounded by sparse plantings and stones or an inn at one of the country's hundreds of hot-spring resorts where the sole purpose is to encourage one to relax while surrounded by nature. Authors Chadine Flood Gong and Lisa Parramore both lived and worked in Japan in the field of education. Chadine lived on a large estate in Denencho-fu in Tokyo, where the full-time gardener introduced her to the beauty of living with Japanese gardens, while Lisa lived in rural Fukushima, which is surrounded by the Japanese Alps and abundant hot springs. It was their everyday encounters with Japanese aesthetics that planted the seeds for the vocations to which they are dedicated today. Like the authors, many of the homeowners whose gardens appear in this book lived in or traveled to Japan, and consequently they enjoy having gardens that remind them of the culture they came to know and love.

The gardens in this book have been selected to inspire you to dream about what is possible for your own living environment. Some of the gardens are created as part of the "home." An ideal Japanese garden is viewed through a window while one relaxes inside, sipping tea at the kitchen table; soaking in a hot bath; or sitting on a bench on a covered veranda. These gardens can be enjoyed even in, or perhaps especially in, inclement weather. Some are elegant ideals on large properties, complete with man-made waterfalls and many tons of rock brought in at great cost. Others were built on a modest budget and require less intensive ongoing care. Some are located on sites already blessed with enviable conditions, such as aged oaks covered with soft moss or natural creeks that need only an old stone lantern to convey the spirit of a Japanese garden. Others are flat suburban spaces with narrow yards, put to good use with large windows that look out onto carefully arranged scenes. Indeed, most people can create a beautiful Japanese garden whether they have a flat suburban lot, a steeply sloped area, or a small balcony. So, pour yourself a cup of tea and relax for an armchair tour of these special spaces of serenity.

A Japanese garden is what makes a house a home. In fact, the word for "home" in Japanese is a combination of two characters: "ka" for house and "tei" for garden.

POOLS OF REFLECTION

For the person who prefers stillness of water to koi and pond plants, a reflecting pool can enhance the impact of carefully chosen land plants and ornaments nearby. This reflecting pool, just $3\frac{1}{2}$ x 12 feet, was embedded in an existing redwood deck next to the home that belongs to Chadine Flood Gong and her husband. Chadine understands the link between interior and exterior spaces. Since the space is restricted to a small deck, she created the narrow reflecting pool.

Located just outside the home's side entry, one can see and enjoy the reflecting pool from the kitchen and dining room and also upon coming and going. Since Chadine prefers

Asymmetric balance, one of the defining characteristics of Japanese aesthetics, is achieved with geometric shapes placed off center.

stillness and tranquility, no pump is used, but water can be easily drained and refilled once a week as the pool is only five inches deep. At a certain time of the day, the sunshine hits the surface of the water and reflects the incredible patterns created by the water's movement on the ceilings of the interior rooms nearby.

The combination of geometric shapes invites closer inspection. The rectangular pool, the square stepping stones placed off center, and the round, antique metal lantern all work together to achieve asymmetric balance, punctuated by the horizontal deck pattern and the black bamboo's vertical lines and their reflection in the water. Owing to its shape, the stone lantern on the deck is known as a kimono sleeve lantern, a copy of the famous one at Arashiyama in Kyoto. The area reflects Chadine's love of Japanese aesthetics and her preference for a minimalist austerity. "I try to create a feeling, not perfection," she says.

This stone lantern is carved like the proportions of a woman's kimono sleeve. Lanterns are decorative elements placed where light is needed or to cast a reflection in water.

MIRRORS IN THE SUN

This courtyard garden in an Eichler-style house has evolved over time to meet the homeowners' needs. After an extensive remodel of the house itself, Dr. Robert Swenson and his wife, Carol, wanted a dramatic entrance that would complete their home's role as a retreat from hectic workdays and yet be interesting enough for their future retirement. They asked Chadine to create their anticipated sanctuary so that it would have a spark of drama yet require minimal maintenance.

With a few strategically placed elements, the atrium was transformed into a welcoming entry imbued with a mood of reverence. The concrete courtyard was replaced with a wooden deck and reflecting pool. Despite the fact that the entire area boasts but one living thing, a single black pine tree, the space has an organic, natural feel. The trio of rocks breaks up the long band of water while two slate stepping stones lead directly over the water to the master bedroom's separate entrance, creating an environment of quiet and welcoming serenity. The couple was delighted with the results, achieved with locally available materials on a modest budget.

Several years later when Carol had more leisure time, she began to give concert parties. The question arose whether the courtyard should be converted to interior space. She

Furu-ike ya
kawazu tobi-komu
mizu-no-oto.
BASHO (1644–1694)

Pond of water
into it goes a frog
splash.

In the courtyard of this Eichler-style house, still water reflects a trio of rocks of varying sizes and shapes. The rocks form an asymmetrical triangle, a common arrangement in Japanese gardens.

contacted Chadine who again came up with a comparatively inexpensive solution that preserved the Japanese garden. A retractable roof made of translucent fiberglass was added over the courtyard for use during the evening concert events and to provide shelter from the sun during the hot days of summer. The retractable roof's grid pattern proved the perfect complement to the home's interior shoji doors.

Slate stepping stones lead across the water to the master suite.

However, since the reflecting pool would now be covered most of the year with the retractable roof, the effect of the humidity from the reflecting pool on the owner's two grand pianos was a concern. Chadine suggested draining the shallow water and filling the pool with gravel and pebbles. One of the enduring aspects of the Japanese garden tradition is that the elements of nature can be symbolized with other materials. Just as a rock is often used to represent a mountain, gravel complemented by rocks is suggestive of a body of water.

In spite of the fact that the problem of humidity for the pianos had been solved, Carol found herself missing the tranquil sight of the water. Some time later, a small pond scene was added in a narrow side yard that can now be seen every day from the kitchen and dining area. The source of recirculating water is camouflaged between two flat rocks, placed one on top of the other. The yukimi-style stone lantern is positioned so that when lighted it is reflected

A retractable roof was added to this courtyard garden to enable the owners to use it as either an area open to the sky or an enclosed room. The grid pattern of the roof echoes the shoji doors of the master bedroom entrance, shown on the previous page.

in the pond. This type of lantern is distinguished by its low profile and wide roof and is traditionally placed near water or an element that is suggestive of water, such as a dry stream. "I love it!" Carol exclaims, welcoming the presence of water once again.

The owner is able to enjoy the tranquil sight of water with this small reflecting pond, which reflects horsetail and a low stone lantern.

INSPIRED BY JAPANESE ART

Nature is a popular theme in Japanese art, particularly in the folding screens that traditionally served as both art and room dividers. Known as *byobu*, these screens were often painted with scenes from poetry and literature. The strength of nature, expressed frequently as a theme in Japanese art and poetry, can also serve as inspiration for Japanese garden design. Other folding screens, such as the smaller tearoom screens, carry simple patterns that reflect common patterns used in Japanese decor. Such subtle patterns made ideal backdrops for seasonal flower arrangements. The outdoor scenes in this chapter were inspired by Japanese art.

Distant scenery, viewed through the gate, is incorporated into this garden, whereas the bridge invites one to venture beyond. This type of zigzag bridge was inspired by the eight-fold bridge in the screen shown on page 21.

IRIS AND BRIDGE BY STREAM

Seen in the photo on the previous page, the plateau, nestled between two forested slopes on Chadine Flood Gong's property, receives little sunshine but many falling leaves each autumn. Rather than tame the wilderness, Chadine recycled construction planks to form an eight-fold bridge, flanked by a stone lantern crouching on the ground. There are a few clumps of irises, and the scenery is intentionally devoid of color and flowers. Viewed from the interior, it quietly suggests humble solitude.

The eight-fold bridge, or *yatsuhashi*, derives from a chapter in the Heian-period (794–1185) literary classic *Tales of Ise*. The poet, an exiled courtier, arrived at the famous bridge and composed a verse. The first syllable of each line together forms the Japanese word for iris (*kakitsubata*):

Karagoromo
kitsutsu narenishi
tsuma shi areba
harubaru kinuru
tabi o shi zo omou.

I have a beloved wife,
familiar as the skirt
of a well-worn robe,
and so this distant journeying
fills my heart with grief.[*]

The marsh, where the waters of a river branched into eight channels, boasted splendid clusters of iris in bloom. Enchanted romantics have been recreating this scene ever since.

---

[*] Helen Craig McCullough, translator, *Tales of Ise: Lyrical Episodes from Tenth Century Japan.* (Stanford, CA: Stanford University Press, 1968), 78.

The planks of the bridge in Chadine's garden, crossing at varying angles, some boards crossing at oblique angles, make an asymmetrical composition. The uncomplicated rendition of this famed bridge came about as a result of Chadine's acquiring a Meiji-era (1868–1912) six-paneled screen, seen here in her bedroom, which depicts irises in bloom, clustered about a multi-planked foot bridge. Only five of the eight sections are seen in this one of a pair of screens; the complete picture is left to the imagination of the viewer. Inside and outside, these artistic expressions are in harmony.

This antique six-panel screen was inspired by an eight-fold bridge, shown on the opening page of this chapter. The eight-fold bridge, or yatsuhashi, as described on the previous page, has inspired numerous artists and gardeners.

A flower bed is converted into an inspired scene in this wood-land landscape. The iris is celebrated in Japan as one of the flowers of summer.

RAFT-STYLE BRIDGE

Soon after Chadine created her *yatsuhashi* scene, Lisa Parramore designed a variation for her mother, Barbara Parramore, who loves irises. Two planks placed at an angle to form a bridge is a popular Japanese design motif, known as a raft-style bridge (*ikada-bashi*), and is another lovely way to enjoy irises. Your legs might brush against the cascading leaves of an iris clump as you make your way across the bridge, or you might find yourself at nearly eye level with the blooms, some of which grow five to six feet tall. *Iris ensata*, which grows in drier conditions, and *iris laevigata*, which thrives in bog gardens or pots placed directly in water, are two species popular in Japanese gardens.

This approach proved ideal for a small garden on Barbara's gently sloped, oak tree–studded property in North Carolina. The site selected for the garden was a long, narrow raised bed that also functions as a retaining wall. As the space did not lend itself to a traditional bridge with eight planks, a simple raft-style bridge was built. The rectangular plot frames a canvas whose view is enjoyed when one is going to and coming from the car as well as from inside the kitchen, where Barbara, a retired professor, eats all but the most formal meals.

The long, narrow plot has two flat bridges connected by three stepping stones. The graceful, sword-like leaves of the Japanese iris are lovely, whether or not the flowers are in bloom. The bridge leads to a Japanese maple and oribe-style lantern, named for the famous tea master and designer Furuta Oribe. The white and gray quartz are native to the land the house was built on. The minerals were left behind millions of years ago when a river ran through the area and washed the soil away. A rolled-bamboo fence conceals the vertical space between the elevated deck and the garden, and the small wing fence provides a pleasing transition between the opaque backdrop of the rolled fence and the openness of the rest of the mature woodland backyard.

A wing fence softens the transition between the deck and garden.

This tearoom screen is low and wide, as its original purpose was to serve as a decorative backdrop for drinking tea while seated on a tatami floor. Here, it is placed on a low tatami platform, a practical substitute in a modern Western room. The platform doubles as a "stage" for the couple's daughter to practice the violin. The screen's checkerboard pattern inspired the granite basin in the garden shown on the next page.

After the irises complete their annual show, the dominant color of this garden is decidedly green. The contrast between the varying shades of green in the plants, the warm tones of the wooden bridge and golden bamboo fence, and the white-gray palate of the stones and lantern makes for a picturesque landscape. Towering oaks filter sunlight, scattering dewy reflections and shadows that might escape notice if a rainbow of colors took center stage. "It's a perfect spot for constant enjoyment," says Barbara. "I find myself peeking out the window more than ever."

CHECKERBOARD PATTERN

Japanese art also inspired the decor of Steve and Patricia Lee Hoffmann's home. Living in Tokyo for four years in the 1990s gave them a taste for Japanese art and design. Back in the United States, when their home was being remodeled, they stressed to Chadine that they liked checkerboard patterns and asked her to incorporate them wherever possible. Chadine acquired a tearoom screen from the Meiji era for the home. The screen features a checkerboard pattern, known in Japanese as *ishidatani*, a pattern traditionally reserved for use by the upper two ranks of court nobility. A similar pattern, referred to as the *ichimatsu* pattern, can be seen at the Shokin-tei Teahouse of the Katsura Imperial Villa in Kyoto.

To echo the screen's pattern, Chadine incorporated the checkerboard motif into the design of a small garden area just outside the living room. She located an unusual cube-shaped granite water basin with a checkerboard pattern. Placed near a pair of French doors in a bed of river pebbles, the basin can be seen from the living room and other rooms in the house. Water flowing into the basin is enjoyed not only by the family but also by the wild birds that are abundant in the area.

A Ginkaku-ji style basin, unusual for its cube shape and checkerboard pattern, attracts the occasional bird. The basin derives its name from the original Edo-period (1600–1858) basin found at Ginkaku-ji, a villa in Kyoto.

*The sight and sound of water flowing into this basin, which is also shown on the previous page,
creates a peaceful feeling in a garden. Placed where one might rinse one's hands,
the basin, known in Japanese as a chōzubachi (literally hand water bowl), is used
today primarily as a decorative element.*

SPECIAL MOMENT, SPECIAL PLACE

The *tokonoma* is a recess in the wall found in the traditional Japanese home and in the teahouse. It is used to display hanging scrolls and other interesting objets d'art. In the teahouse behind the home of Ren Brown and Robert DeVee, a scroll of elegant calligraphic *kanji* reads "ichi-go, ichi-e," which means "special moment, special place." An expression that acknowledges the transient quality of the human experience, it urges tea ceremony host and guest to savor each encounter as if it were their last.

A self-described third-generation Japanophile, Ren Brown is the son of a professor of Japanese history and the grandson of a missionary to Japan. Together with artist Robert DeVee, Ren owns a

The scroll seen at the back of the room displays calligraphy that reads "special moment, special place," which is a metaphor for the way of tea and of life.

The phrase *ichi-go, ichi*-e means "special moment, special place." Every occasion of extending hospitality to another person is a particular occasion never to recur in one's lifetime, so one should try to make it perfect.

gallery in Bodega Bay, California, that specializes in contemporary Japanese art, the work of local artists, and antique Japanese furniture.

There is much to savor in this home, as the art experts have endeavored to create memorable vignettes that express their warm hospitality, beginning in the gallery itself, housed in what was once, in part, an attached garage. Rather than fill in an existing opening in the garage door, the art dealers fashioned a petite garden featuring a moss-covered stone water basin just outside. By making use of this low "window," wall space is preserved for artwork while this unexpected view delights patrons of the gallery. Nineteenth-century scientist and pioneer Edward S. Morse, who marveled in his book *Japanese Homes and their Surroundings* at the ability of the Japanese to develop the narrowest plots of ground "solely for the benefit of the room within," would be pleased to see this concept so well executed here. A single fresh blossom placed upon the water basin reminds one of the present season.

Creating a scene from the tiniest patch of ground is a hallmark of Japanese garden design.

Behind the gallery, the grounds of the residence give rise to more special moments, such as the occasional tea ceremony or a friend's impromptu practice of the *shakuhachi*, a traditional flute made of bamboo. A dry stream follows the gentle slope of the land, flanked by attractive evergreen shrubs, pines, and a few drifts of wildflowers. So natural looking is the dry stream that once in a while a guest has been known to ask where the water is—a compliment to Gregory Powers, who was instrumental in bringing the garden together. Following the path of stepping stones, one eventually arrives at a waiting bench, or *machiai*, to relax while enjoying the garden, or, when the actual tea ceremony is held, to wait for the host to escort guests into the teahouse. The wall of the machiai was constructed of heavy plywood, layered with chicken wire and felt paper, and finished with stucco.

Robert conceived the teahouse himself, rendering a three-dimensional model to convey his vision to a local carpenter. "Never have I worked on something with

The circular window of the machiai, or waiting bench, was cut to fit a silkworm basket. A bamboo basket used for collecting garden debris is stowed next to the bench.

The teahouse has sliding shoji doors as well as exterior removable doors, which allow the structure to be used in various weather conditions.

quite as much intent," he said. The customary low door was omitted in favor of a design that allowed the garden to be enjoyed while sitting inside on the tatami, mats made of woven straw. While the 9 x 9–foot tearoom adheres to local building codes, an L-shaped veranda, or *engawa*, makes the tearoom look and feel more spacious. It also has removable doors to protect the fragile tatami from the elements.

The miniature teahouse, rendered with chopsticks, allowed the owners to communicate their wishes to local carpenters.

An engawa, a narrow, covered veranda that runs along the length of a home's exterior, extends the house and frames the view.

The front entrance of the house, reached via carefully placed stepping stones and a handsome entry gate, is flanked to the right by yet another garden, the focus of which is a pond stocked with vibrant koi. Viewed from the covered veranda or the kitchen, flowering shrubs provide bursts of color in the spring while a large shrub, known as a Harry Lauder's walking stick, presents a hauntingly gnarled form in winter. The wide eave, supported by vertical posts, frames and contrasts with the motion of the waterfall and swimming koi to create a living work of art.

Swimming koi add color and movement to this lushly landscaped water garden.

An abstract composition gets its inspiration from the dry sand-and-stone gardens in Japan.

Tucked behind the house is a dry sand-and-stone garden, inspired by the *karesansui*, or dry landscape, gardens in Japan. This abstract garden is intended to be viewed from multiple stations and elevations. Relatively lightweight volcanic rocks were selected for their beauty as well as ease of handling. Robert rakes the wave-like patterns in a particular form of crushed granite sold as poultry grit about once every six weeks. Some consider the raking of sand to be an active form of meditation, and the overall effect of the dry garden is one of quiet reflection.

GARDEN FOR IKEBANA

Perched high in the foothills of the Santa Cruz Mountains, Martin Herbach and Elaine Sakamoto enjoy a breathtaking view of the valley below from their home. They invited award-winning landscape-designer David Kato to create the feeling of a Japanese garden to complement their Craftsman-style home.

Though the choice of plants for the landscape was necessarily limited to those that are deer resistant, some unusual trees made the cut. A Japanese maple, known as *koto no ito* for the resemblance of its soft, threadlike foliage to the strings of the harp-like *koto*, graces the entrance. In the rear garden, Martin points out a summer-blooming

A Japanese maple, known in Japan as koto no ito momiji, is so named for the resemblance of its foliage to the koto, a stringed instrument similar to a harp.

camellia, said to be special because Buddha died beneath a pair of such trees.[1]

Dedicated students of the Ikenobo School of Ikebana for the past twenty years, the couple has traveled twice to Kyoto for intensive hands-on seminars. They use the leaves of ferns, heavenly bamboo, pines, and native plants from their garden for their biweekly ikebana arrangements.

The Ikenobo School, dating back to the fifteenth century, focuses on two forms of flower arranging. The older form, *rikka*, is similar to the art of bonsai in that it permits the use of wires to bend and shape the plant material. Although it is awe inspiring to work on this art form that has remained unchanged for more than six centuries, Elaine prefers the more recent form, *shoka shimputai*, in which all things must look natural and the use of wires is not permitted. Serious study of shoka shimputai, Martin explains, requires one to be intimately familiar with how plants grow in the wild, so that branches that weep naturally are selected to play that role in flower arrangements. Martin's detailed knowledge of plants from his study of ikebana clearly informs the ongoing care and evolution of the garden.

Above: Rikka form of ikebana—with the exception of the iris, all material for this arrangement was selected from the garden.

Right: Shoka shimputai form of ikebana—the gravelia blossom, pine candles, and cycad leaf are all from the garden.

---

[1] The summer-blooming camellia, or *natsutsubaki* in Japanese, is a stand-in for the sallow, which does not grow in Japan. Buddha died beneath a pair of sallowood trees in India, but Japanese poets have referred to the natsutsubaki as *sarasoju*, which translates as twin sallows.

This hillside garden, adorned with a mix of conifers and native plants, provides a variety of material that the owners use in their ikebana arrangements.

Martin particularly enjoys experimenting with native plants.

David Kato, who founded his design-build firm Katoscapes in 1983, approaches the gardens he designs as a composer would a piece of music. "The plants," says Kato, "they're like music, like key notes, each plant associated with a certain note, and when it's composed and put together, you have a song. Plant composition is my music."

In springtime, this composition of purple, blue, and green blankets the steep hillside and caresses a soothing waterfall. This gentle palette, accentuated by the constant sound of water, offers a lovely backdrop and a place where Elaine likes

Wochi-kochi ni
taki no oto kiku
wakaba kana.
—Buson (1716–1784)

Young leaves—
the sound of a waterfall
heard from here and yonder.

Waterfalls are frequently incorporated into Japanese gardens for their beauty as well as their pleasing sounds.

to relax. Referring to how a garden allows his clients to experience nature, Kato explains, "Once the mind gets quiet and still, then one can feel the qualities of the garden." That serene feeling is one reason Martin and Elaine spend a great deal of time in their garden. Elaine says, "One never gets tired of this view."

ROOMS WITH A VIEW

The Japanese garden tradition perfected the art of bringing the outside in long before it became fashionable elsewhere. Homes designed in Japan for maximum ventilation during hot, humid summers had large, removable sliding doors that often exposed an entire wall to the scenery outside. During this modern age of air-conditioning, floor-to-ceiling windows and sliding glass doors play a similar role without the daily chore of removing and storing the doors.

Viewing a garden while relaxing inside—sitting at the *kotatsu*, a low table common in Japanese homes; in a Western living room nestled in a favorite couch or armchair; or even lounging in the bath—may

This rain chain, unusual in its shape and color, guides rain to a dry stream of river pebbles.

well be the ultimate Japanese garden experience. While it is true that a well-designed small garden can create the biggest visual impact, more often than not the reverse is true for the window. Usually the larger the window, the better, regardless of the size of available land outside. The following three gardens, adjacent to the homes' most-used rooms, demonstrate this concept.

A PLACE TO WATCH THE RAIN

Takatoro
hiru wa monouki
hashira kana.
—SENNA (1650–1723)

The tall stone lantern,
in the light of day
is a pillar of loneliness.

The room where Chadine Flood Gong and her husband spend most of their free time features a wall of glass that separates the room from the narrow pathway that she turned into a garden for the display of a

A historic lantern, carved with a chrysanthemum motif that is commonly used by the imperial family of Japan, anchors the view from a glass-walled room.

*When the garden is brought right up to the house, nature's
ability to nourish is immediately accessible.*

rare and historic Japanese stone lantern. The lantern, carved with a chrysanthemum motif, was sent by the Japanese Imperial Government to San Francisco
for the 1915 Panama Pacific Exposition. Although never actually lit, the prized
stone lantern is placed where light would be needed—in this case next to
stepping stones and a wooden bridge pathway.

Golden bamboo forms a sheltering forest of privacy for the glass-
walled room. The lower leaves of the bamboo have been stripped to enhance the beauty of the trunks. The chain hanging from the eaves serves
as a rainwater conductor to the pebble-filled stream below. For Chadine
and her husband, rain is never as beautiful as when it comes down the
chain, seen from the interior. Inside the room, a Japanese scroll painting of sprouting bamboo was intentionally selected to echo the bamboo
grove outside.

A PLACE TO HEAL

The garden of Katherine Lee Gong provides a faithful backdrop for everyday
living and is a source of mental healing. The living room furniture is arranged
so one can take in the view, and the garden is also visible while Kate goes

about her daily activities. "I enjoy looking down and seeing the water through the missing planks," says Kate, explaining that when she had the bridge rebuilt she kept the same pattern. Intentionally omitting planks from a bridge is in keeping with the Japanese inclination to find beauty in imperfection. "It's perfectly imperfect," says Chadine, Kate's sister-in-law.

The beauty of the bridge lies in the incompleteness of the planks.

Japanese-style gardens, inherently tranquil, invite spiritual nourishment and healing. Kate recalls how her late husband, in his last few months, maneuvered himself in his wheelchair to the window to look out to the pond every morning. As a physician, he was well aware that his death was near, yet here, in the room with a view of the pond, he was at peace with his dying. Seeing the garden and knowing how much it meant to her husband has helped Kate heal.

The depth produced by the water's reflection makes this garden feel larger than its actual footprint of about one hundred square feet. The garden is built onto the roof of the extended basement below. Lined with concrete, the pool holding the water is close to the house but poses no threat, and a supply of minnows ensures mosquitoes are kept at bay. A single pine and Japanese maple are mature enough to require minimal pruning, and moss grows naturally on the island rock during the rainy season and with Kate's help during the dry summer months.

A Place to Relax

When Lisa Parramore lived in rural Fukushima in northern Japan in the 1990s, she spent many weekdays trudging through the snow and many weekends skiing. To warm up, she soaked either in one of the area's abundant natural hot springs or in her apartment's small but deep soaking tub. So soothing did she find the bathing customs in Japan that she vowed that if she ever got the chance to design her own bathroom, it would have a soaking tub with a view. Many years later, she realized that dream. The master bathroom in the home she shares with her husband and their two children, Alec and Luke, has a thirty-four-inch deep circular soaking tub adjacent to a large picture window.

Although the bathroom faces a narrow, 6^1/$_2$-foot-wide side yard that functions as a service path, one is aware only of a beautifully pruned Japanese black pine. Framed by the oversized window and blind, which Lisa chose for its similarity in texture to rice paper, the tree brings the intimacy of nature to daily bathing. A simple reed fence camouflages the ordinary dividing fence they

A Japanese black pine, its size appropriate for the large picture window, is on view from a deep soaking tub.

share with the property next door and provides a backdrop for the container-grown black pine. Whether the couple is getting ready for the workday or winding down in the evening with their children, the beauty of nature is close at hand.

PRIVATE
SANCTUARIES

In medieval Japan, small enclosed gardens were first built to create scenes that could be enjoyed from a building's interior. These small gardens were appreciated for their close-up views of nature, even by people who could afford to landscape much larger spaces. Particular attention was paid to the artful arrangement of rocks.

The small courtyard garden, known as *tsuboniwa*, later became a common fixture in the townhouses of Kyoto. In densely populated Japan, tsuboniwa can be found today in homes, restaurants, office buildings, and hotels. Given that residential land is increasingly at a premium, the tsuboniwa style offers one the opportunity to create a private sanctuary.

The undulating shoreline of the gravel "sea" softens the home's abundant right angles.

Watching the Bamboo Grow

Inazuma ni
koboruru oto ya
take no tsuyu.
—Buson (1716–1784)

Lightning flashes—
the drops of dew
spill down the bamboo.

High-tech industry managers Jonathan Davidson and Erica Schroeder, new owners of a 1960s Joseph Eichler house, asked Lisa Parramore to create a garden in their atrium that started out, in Erica's words, as a "grim cement wasteland." The atrium consists of floor-to-ceiling glass on three sides, a popular feature of Eichler homes, so the space is in full view from the rooms where the couple, thirteen-year-old Megan, and six-year-old Ethan, do most of their living. When Jon confessed that he had a miniature zen tray garden on his desk at work, Lisa immediately began to picture an abstract scene that would evoke a certain mood and complement the couple's contemporary art and furnishings in the interior.

The one solid wall was selected as a backdrop for black bamboo, a plant that intrigued the homeowners for its form and color. Bamboo was planted so that it would grow up towards the sky in the rectangular space created by the eaves and roofline. Black bamboo is a particularly attractive species in that its young culms are green, gradually turning mottled purple and finally a striking ebony. During the spring growth season, the bamboo's underground rhizomes send forth new shoots that literally grow up to a foot per day until reaching their ultimate height in about six weeks. While visually dominating

A sleeve fence, typically used to visually link the architecture to the garden, serves to partially conceal a bedroom entrance.

because of its height, the bamboo's slender culms and lacy leaves are light enough to move and rustle in the wind.

"It's tempting for people to make this kind of space 'functional' with tables and chairs, but I took my cue from Erica, who indicated that spillover seating for the occasional cocktail party might suffice," says Lisa. A slate-veneered wall serves that purpose, frames the bamboo, and helps camouflage the necessary root barrier, which prevents the bamboo's spread to unwanted areas. Sunlight during the day and low-voltage lighting at night produce delicate shadows on the wall. The height and the movement of the bamboo provide relief from the horizontal lines of the roof and interesting boardwalk. The den adjacent to the garden quickly became the preferred place to be.

To add subtle definition to the remaining vertical space without blocking the view of the bamboo, a columnar stone fountain and a sleeve fence were selected. The fountain serves as a focal point when the front door is opened, and it also infuses the space with the pleasant sound of trickling water.

The stone fountain is the first thing the owners see when they open the front door. "It's like my own private sanctuary," says owner Jon.

The sleeve fence, or *sodegaki,* is made of split bamboo; it derives its name from its resemblance to the sleeve of a woman's kimono. The fence provides a subtle partition between the wooden walkway made of *ipé,* a Brazilian hardwood, leading to the entrance of the house proper and the sliding glass door of one of the bedrooms. It also marks the beginning of a secondary path to the wall where the owners enjoy taking a closer look at the progress of the bamboo's new shoots in springtime. The stepping-stone path, composed of cut Connecticut bluestone, appears to float above the ground, and its diagonal layout echoes the subtle zigzag of the walkway.

The quantity and variety of plants were intentionally limited. Potted horsetail, planted along the walkway between the front door and the atrium, foreshadows the bamboo. Heavenly bamboo, *sasa veitchii,* and ferns were chosen for their lacy texture. The rocks that anchor the garden lend a permanent counterpoint to the graceful plants.

"Our house has been transformed into a peaceful oasis," says Erica. "One of the most surprising things to me was how simple the garden appears at the outset

Typical Japanese ornaments give depth to a small space. This is a photo of the garden as it appeared immediately after it was built.

and yet how day by day different aspects make themselves visible so that you wind up with a fairly complicated and yet soothing mental image. It is a fascinating mix of form, texture, and material."

NAMASTE

The small, intimate tsuboniwa-style garden makes an ideal atmosphere for the practice of yoga. Randee Seiger asked Chadine Flood Gong to design a garden for an approximately 11 x 3 1/2–foot rectangular patch of ground adjacent to an existing deck that she uses for practicing yoga. This enclosed garden is visible from the master suite and attached library.

In this case, the garden's purpose is beauty rather than function. The area is separated from the outside by a fence and the side of the house. There are two ways of approaching—from the interior of the house via the deck and from the backyard. A Japanese-style gate was built to enclose the path from the garden. Stepping stones lead from this gate to the stone water basin, the only focal point of the garden. The variety of shrubs is kept to a minimum: a few heavenly bamboo and a Japanese maple are planted to the side and behind the water basin for height. Also, to tone down the dark color of the home's siding, a light-colored wing fence is placed to the right. The gravel is a somber color to match the dark color of the fence and the exterior of the house. The ceramic black jar serves as a reminder to rid oneself of mental clutter prior to beginning a session of yoga.

A year after installation of the small garden, Randee finds that the space fulfills its intended purpose: "It is peaceful and serene," she says.

Some years later, the garden is still a calm oasis where the owner practices yoga.

SKYSCAPE IN SILHOUETTE

What would a Japanese garden feel like if it were at the top of the world? The garden behind the home of Dr. Walter and Lisa Kran gives the impression of being just that. What stands between their house and the sprawling valley below is a finely manicured panorama of conifers and evergreen shrubs. The exceptional skyscape surrounds the gentle sounds of a waterfall that the couple enjoys from their bedroom on warm nights.

Finely pruned evergreen trees and shrubs are often employed to give a Japanese garden its structure.

Kururu ma wa
chitose wo sugusu
kokochi shite
matsu wa makoto ni
hisashikarikeri.
—Anonymous

[ ]

Aching nostalgia—
as evening darkens
and every moment
grows
longer and longer,
I feel
ageless as the
thousand year pine.

Two years of military service in the Far East and several subsequent trips to Japan gave Walter a taste for the aesthetics used in gardens there. "I like the clean lines; the garden gives a relaxing, soothing feeling," he says of the vista above the valley.

The garden, built by the late nurseryman and bonsai-expert Jimmy Inadame thirty-five years ago, has aged well, thanks to continued grooming and care. He used lava rock to carve the stone lantern and supporting stones for the waterfall. Generous stepping stones made from hand-set pebbles embedded in mortar connect the house to the garden.

But it's the carefully pruned plantings that stand out and make this garden a fine example of the use of human scale. The plantings consist mostly of evergreen trees and shrubs that provide interest year-round. A strict adherence to Japanese design principles relegates taller shade trees, if they are used, to a background role, while trees that contribute to the garden scene are pruned so that they can be enjoyed at eye level. Skilled pruning also enhances the forms of the trees, showing their trunks and branches to best advantage.

*Kenneth Rexroth, *One Hundred More Poems from the Japanese* (New York: New Directions Publishing, 1974), 82.

A striking deodar cedar, in silhouette at sunset, watches over the garden.

Well-placed boulders camouflage the source of the waterfall.

Preserving the Past

In contrast to the style of *tsuboniwa*, the aristocratic gardens of the Heian era (794–1185) sprawled across the grounds of palaces and amused the leisure class. Originally large enough to be viewed from a boat, the so-called hill-and-pond style was gradually reduced in size and came to be known as the stroll-style garden. Park-like, this type could be used to describe many public Japanese gardens in the West and is what many Westerners think of when they imagine a typical Japanese garden. At its best, it invites one into a sensory experience in which man-made hills and skillful plantings hide and reveal each successive view, enjoyed while one strolls across paths and bridges.

The approach to the De Sabla Japanese Tea Garden leads to a handsome pillared gate, typical of the finer country estates of Japan.

The De Sabla Japanese Tea Garden, one of the oldest extant Japanese gardens in the West, is listed on the National Register of Historic Places.

Ever since Japan opened up to the West in 1868, a small number of determined Americans with means and passion have erected impressive Japanese-style stroll gardens on their American estates. Achili and Joan Paladini are the current owners of one of the oldest extant examples of such a garden, the story of which began when a wealthy American widower sailed for Japan in 1893.

Henry Pike Bowie, founder and first president of the Japan Society of the United States, had this teahouse and stroll garden built on his property, which now straddles the California cities of Hillsborough and San Mateo. Bowie spent many years in Kyoto, mastering the language and customs of Japan; he also became recognized as a skilled brush painter. Bowie commissioned Makoto Hagiwara, the landscape designer of San Francisco's Golden Gate Park, to create this beautiful retreat. Artificial hills, known in Japanese as *tsukiyama*, surround a wide pond, which casts beautiful reflections of the teahouse. Named *Higurashi-en*, or "a garden worthy of a day's contemplation," the garden satisfies with the three basic elements: plants, rocks, and water. Reflecting in the pond are shapely evergreen shrubs and specimen trees with twisted trunks and fine foliage.

A stone bridge links the island to the rest of the garden, said to be several hundred years

Maiko, one of Henry Pike Bowie's many paintings on silk, is the Japanese term for a geisha apprentice.

A centuries-old stone bridge bears the inscription, "The bridge to eternal tranquility."

old, while rare materials from Japan, such as petrified lava, that are no longer available for export remind one of what a unique landscape this is. Horatio S. Stoll, writing for *House Beautiful* in 1914, likened the scene to "a dream of fairyland come true." California history, too, lives on in the two-hundred-year-old triple laceleaf Japanese maple and other artifacts from the 1915 Pan Pacific Exposition.

The estate later became the property of industrialist Eugene de Sabla Jr., and today the garden bears his name. The estate was subdivided, and the teahouse became a full-time private residence in 1946. A large wing was added to make the teahouse more suitable as a residence. It has served as the Paladinis' home for the past eighteen years. Through Joan's efforts, the teahouse and garden have been restored and the property has been placed on the National Register of Historic Places. Besides doing some of the pruning, which she enjoys, Joan spends time in the garden watching and feeding several koi, two of whom she has named Kira and Liberace. "No matter where you

Hashi fumeba
uo shizumikeri
haru no mizu.
SHIKI (1866—1902)

Stepping on the bridge,
the fish disappear:
spring water.

A triple laceleaf Japanese maple dates back to the 1915 Pan Pacific Exposition.

Above: An angled wing, added to the teahouse after it became a private residence, helps the home embrace the garden.

Right: A pair of mallard ducks suns themselves on the "feeding stone," which one stands on to feed the koi.

stand, there's not one bad view," says Joan. Neighbors drop by with leftover bread for the ducks who compete with two resident racing greyhounds for the choice spot to sit and sun, a koi "feeding stone" set a bit out from the pond's banks. Joan's grandchildren also enjoy playing in the garden. "They love Easter egg hunts here." Indeed, thanks to Joan's efforts, this Japanese garden will hide and reveal its surprises for generations to come.

Dry Landscape Meets Modern Minimalism

Successful minimalist design requires careful placement of each element used in the garden, including empty space itself. The garden style known as *karesansui* is characterized by the use of rocks, gravel, and few, if any, plants to compose an abstract scene. A single viewing position is typical, and the absence of clutter encourages contemplation.

COURTYARD GARDEN

The walls of this six-month-old condominium courtyard garden that Chadine Flood Gong designed provide enclosure and a clean backdrop for a Japanese maple, heavenly bamboo, and a few stands of black bamboo. Several cement squares were removed to create an

To the Japanese garden designer, an unadorned blank wall is a canvas on which to highlight a choice specimen tree, such as this Japanese maple.

asymmetrical layout. Placing a simple path of stones and a wooden bridge at an angle suggests tension, while a stone lantern and rain chain in the foreground provide the illusion of greater depth.

The owner enjoys the view from the living room, kitchen, and dining area, as the entire wall consists of floor-to-ceiling windows. The privacy affords the owner a place for Jaeger, her sleek greyhound, to be given a bath or simply run about though still confined within the walls of her condominium. The small stone *gorintou*, sometimes used as a funerary monument, stands in memory of the owner's late companion, Argos, a racing greyhound.

That the garden essentially takes care of itself is a gift for a busy professional in the midst of a career change. Keeping weeds pulled and thinning out the bamboo once a year are all that are necessary to maintain the garden's tidy appearance.

Empty space defines this minimalist courtyard garden while the stone lantern grounds the viewer's position.

The artifacts in this courtyard were selected to create a minimalist feeling and also as a practical matter. At a vacation home, there is little time to properly care for plants.

A GARDEN WITHOUT PLANTS

Concrete patios bordered by planting squares need not play host to plants. Their geometric shapes can frame carefully selected accents. Here, an entry courtyard to Chadine's beach house received a makeover when the coastal climate was found to be inhospitable to plants. She also wanted a vacation home that didn't require much maintenance. On one side, a stone lantern rests in a bed of river pebbles while two cement pavers placed off center add interest. The gray river pebbles are used to reduce the glare of sunlight and to bring out the Japanese aesthetics. A granite bench welcomes travelers and provides a place for them to remove their shoes before entering the house. The rain chain and interior shoji panel draw one's eye up and away from the cement and direct the gaze to the ocean beyond. While tending to plants is one of gardening's pleasures, as this garden shows plants can be eliminated when circumstances necessitate without sacrificing the garden's tranquil qualities.

Designed without plants, the courtyard shown on the previous page ensures that the visitor to this seaside vacation home can relax and enjoy the ocean.

WABI IN THE WILDERNESS

"A Japanese garden is like a haiku poem," says Mark Bourne, a landscape designer who apprenticed in Kyoto. "It reduces the complexity of the natural world to its essence in the garden." For four years, Mark's rigorous training included work on new gardens at Kodai-ji Zen Temple in Japan; pruning at the Kyoto Imperial Palace and the Katsura Detached Palace; and the construction of a Japanese garden in Florence, Italy. As anyone who has spent several years in Japan knows, it is sometimes difficult to convey to others the impact of one's experience there. Mark completed a demanding apprenticeship in a field characterized by strict hierarchy and tradition. As Mark

A dry cascade of pebbles simulates a mountain stream as if it were a natural part of the landscape.

talks about his life's passion, he is clearly informed by the masters who preceded him. One minute he's quoting the *Sakuteiki*, the eleventh-century treatise on Japanese garden design, while the next he's describing the distinctively Japanese awareness of the seasons by reciting a verse by the famous poet Matsuo Basho:

Shizukasa ya
iwa ni shimiiru
semi no koe.
MATSUO BASHO (1644–1694)

Silence:
the sound of the cicadas
sinks into the stone.

Like Basho's haiku, which conjures up the image and sounds of a warm summer's night with a mere seventeen syllables, Mark looks to the vast California wilderness and selects just the right elements that bring local beauty into his clients' lives. Through his company, Windsmith Design, Mark brings his training to bear on an emerging field that combines sophisticated design and pruning techniques with the use of native plants. Just as the Japanese have refined their sculpting methods to produce trees that appear as if they have been shaped by the forces of nature, a new generation of Americans is looking to their own local plant communities for materials that respond to the same care and produce the same elegant results. Sometimes replacing the more familiar imports, coast live oak, western redbud, and the coffeeberry shrub are just a few species being planted in today's Japanese-style gardens.

In a redwood forest on a peak of the Santa Cruz Mountains in Woodside, California, the skyline of San Francisco is visible on a clear day. Having purchased an Asian-inspired home they had admired for many years, Frank and Betsy Stockdale asked Mark to gently tame the weedy hillside that their home and deck overlook.

For Mark, utilizing native plants in the garden is a way to capture the feeling of *wabi*, a poetic sense of desolation that characterized tea garden culture during the sixteenth century. Tea huts of the day were located outside the cities and were suggestive of a rustic retreat far removed from the bustle of urban life. Amid this desolate seclusion, the tea masters developed "an acute sensitivity to nature and the effect of the seasons on the natural world," says Mark. "I am trying to capture the poetic sensitivity to natural beauty of the tea masters."

Mark first reshaped the land. Working around the buttress roots of a huge fir tree, Mark created a plateau and constructed a dry stream that flows across and down the slope of the property. The boulders that flank the edges of the dry stream bed appear to direct the course of the stream as it winds. The planting palette, featuring scrub oaks, manzanitas, and a madrone tree, was selected for its deer resistance and to harmonize with the colors of the surrounding forest. "We're very happy with it," says Betsy.

Each rock was set by hand using a tripod, the traditional method of rock setting still taught in Japanese gardening apprenticeships.

The result of Mark's efforts is a landscape in which one cannot tell where the garden begins and where the wilderness ends.

A Teahouse in the Forest

Sabi, a term that conveys the serenity found in the feeling of loneliness, is used in conjunction with wabi to characterize the mood sought by the early practitioners of tea ceremony. Guests invited to drink tea began their journey to the teahouse on a stepping-stone path that meandered gradually from public space towards the more intimate destinations of a waiting bench and the teahouse, where the host would prepare tea according to strictly prescribed ritual. The image of the simple tea hut in the wilderness, isolated from everyday life, held appeal then and holds appeal now as a temporary reprieve from ordinary business. The tea ceremony itself is a sensory experience in which the host and guests enjoy drinking tea, eating sweets, and savoring the ambiance.

When Dr. Eliot Finkle and his wife, Betty, bought their ranch-style home in 1975, there was an unfinished detached outbuilding in the back of the property. The original owner of the house had lived in Japan and found Japanese aesthetics appealing. Back in the United States, he envisioned a Japanese teahouse, with a floor plan that would accommodate traditional tatami mats of woven straw. The owner's son began construction of the teahouse, but the teahouse was yet to be finished when the Finkles bought the property.

Several years after the Finkles moved in, Chadine Flood Gong introduced Betty to Japanese aesthetics. The small building out back was an ideal teahouse, a small hut in the shadow of a forest under large oak and pine trees. The interior of the teahouse was remodeled so that the Finkles could use it as a retreat and/or guest house. The setting was cultivated to remain forest like, and the approach to the teahouse was adorned with a natural stone lantern and stepping stones embedded deep in the ground. The path to the teahouse is reminiscent of the *roji*, the dewy path that encourages a sense of leaving the

The feeling of wabi-sabi, once sought by tea practitioners who desired an experience removed from materialism, is conveyed by surrounding the teahouse with nature and humanizing the space with simple artifacts.

outside world and entering a special place deep within nature. A stone water basin was placed by the entrance to the teahouse to remind guests to symbolically cleanse their minds of worldly troubles before entering.

A yukata-clad swimmer retreats to the guesthouse, which was originally built as a teahouse in this forest-like setting.

When a swimming pool was built, a Japanese small stone *gorintou*, literally a five-ringed tower with five parts representative of earth, water, fire, wind, and air, was placed so its shadow would be cast in the water of the pool.

The place reminds one of an old Japanese poem:

Miwataseba
hana mo momiji mo
nakarikeri
ura no tomoya no
aki no yugure.

In this wide landscape
I see no cherry blossoms
and the crimson leaves
even in autumn over
a straw-thatched hut by the way.[*]

WABI IN THE WINTERTIME

If wabi-sabi were a season, it would be winter. High above the enchanted city of Santa Fe stands a destination that blends earthy southwestern architecture with rustic Japanese charm. Modeled after the hot-spring resorts found throughout the volcanic archipelago of Japan, *Ten Thousand Waves* is a spa that caters to those seeking the restorative benefits of soaking while surrounded by the wilderness.

Dreaming of a name that would evoke the image of water, the phrase *ten thousand waves* came to Duke Klauck, founder and owner of the Japanese-style spa.

---

[*] Wybe Kuitert, *Themes in the History of Japanese Garden Art* (Honolulu, University of Hawaii Press, 2002), 206.

Fortuitously, a Buddhist monk explained that "one wave, ten thousand waves" is the literal translation of an old zen saying *hitotsu no nami, ma nami,* which suggests "it's all the same, so don't worry." A relaxing soak in one of the outdoor tubs tempts one to take this phrase to heart.

Nature is wild and barely tamed in the forest that surrounds the dozen suites, featuring Japan-inspired decor, that house overnight guests. Nestled in these woods is Crescent Moon, a suite that features its own private courtyard. In this walled garden, the vertical lines of a Japanese-inspired gate contrast with the curves of the adobe building, originally built in the 1930s. Thick adobe walls ensure a sense of enclosure while a hardy cottonwood tree and small piñon tree stand up to the harsh desert climate. Out of respect for the desert climate of the Sangre de Cristo Mountains, architecture and man-made ornaments take

The desolate winter landscape is a metaphor for wabi-sabi, an aesthetic framework that honors the cycle of life and death to which all things are subject.

Winter's first snow falls on this courtyard garden. A gate made of native spruce contrasts with the smooth adobe walls of the landscape.

An informal flagstone path leads to the courtyard garden shown on the previous page. The sides of the path were left intentionally jagged to give the space a rustic feeling.

precedence over the cultivation of plants. "Whatever grows, grows," shrugs Sherie Land, who has gardened here for nearly twenty years. Indeed, the desolation of the desert in wintertime lends itself to the Japanese aesthetic of wabi, a feeling the hot-spring goers of Japan have known for centuries.

CREATED SCENERY

An international attorney and a newspaper editor had long been interested in Japanese gardens, design, and culture. This interest was solidified during the four years the couple lived in Tokyo in a house surrounded by tall timber bamboo. After resettling in the United States, they desired a Japanese garden that would reflect this aesthetic.

Located in a mature neighborhood, the stately 1930s home built in the French provincial style of architecture would not at first glance seem to suggest the use of a Japanese approach to landscaping. However, the couple hired Chadine Flood Gong to do just that, as they had been pleased with the garden she had designed for their previous

A flagstone path with an unexpected jog defines the front lawn and embraces the home's formal appearance. Known as a nobedan, this type of formal path is noted for its juxtaposition of straight lines and irregular shapes.

A stepping-stone path winds through a verdant carpet of baby's tears, which flourishes in the shade of the bamboo.

Harusame ya
utsukushiu naru
mono bakari.
CHIYO-NI (1703–1775)

Spring rain:
everything becomes
more beautiful.

home. First, Chadine designed a flag-stone path made from Connecticut bluestone. Known in Japanese as a *nobedan*, such stone paths are attractive for their juxtaposition of geometry and irregularity.

The remodel opened up the interior to more natural light and incorporated windows to be located for optimal viewing of the garden. The mullioned windows, while adhering to the traditional architectural style of the house, play a vital role in creating scenery for the family members inside. A narrow side yard is a common feature found in today's suburban lots, and the view from inside often starts out as an uninteresting dividing fence. The library window was positioned so that from his reading chair, the husband is able to look out into the side yard. Garden artifacts, namely stone lanterns, a stone water basin, and stepping stones, were recycled from the previous garden. As one looks out at the bamboo moving in the wind and its shadow on the ground and listens to the soothing sound of water flowing into the basin, the garden feels like a peaceful extension of the library.

The plain and expansive sidewall of the garage is visible from the family room and library. Instead of trying to hide the wall, Chadine incorporated it into the total design of the back garden by treating the wall as a canvas for painting or as a Japanese screen. One lone deodar cedar was planted next to a piece of flat stone placed vertically to bring into view its unusual shape.

The miniature fence, constructed from a single bamboo trunk, is just high enough to conceal a water spigot and hose. Such ingenious screening devices are a hallmark of Japanese garden design. A similar fence appears in the photograph on page 61.

A playhouse for the couple's young daughter is placed so the parents can see the girl from inside the house. To create an interesting journey and cozy atmosphere for her, a low fence enclosure and a simple wooden bridge that crosses a dry stream were added. Here, a good-sized boulder, retained from the garden of the former house, became a special sitting place for the playhouse's young owner and occasionally for her mother. The dry stream that flows by the playhouse meanders around much of the yard from its source at the stone basin.

Indeed, this garden shows that the outdoors can be brought inside and that one can happily live with a Japanese-style garden regardless of the style of the house.

A bridge invites the imagination into a child's playhouse, which is partially concealed by a wooden fence. This style of fence is characteristically Japanese and is easy to construct with locally available materials.

A Garden for All Seasons

A couple with a fondness for Asian art began to develop a Japanese-style stroll garden once their children were grown. A dozen truckloads of dirt were hauled in to fill in the backyard pool and create a slope that would form the primary backdrop for the new landscape. Shaping the land this way allows for more generous plantings, and it also provides serene views from several perspectives from the home's second floor. The main formal path cuts diagonally across the garden, leading to a pergola-covered deck, which echoes the neutral brown of the L-shaped ranch-style house. A number of old Japanese ornaments reveals the couple's love of Asian objets d'art,

Cherry blossoms scatter across this stroll garden, which is enveloped by spring color.

such as several aged stone lanterns and an unusual roof tile engraved with a dragon's face that marks the path's beginning.

A rich canvas of conifers and several varieties of clumping bamboo ensure that there will be visual interest year-round, while Japanese maples and flowering cherries take center stage during spring. Starting with three bonsai ponderosa pines, purchased from the caretaker of a nearby public Japanese garden, the owners grew their collection by searching out specimens near and far. "It used to be easier to find good pines," remarks the physician-owner who has devoted many leisure hours over the past fifteen years to creating this exceptional landscape, but these days he relies on an out-of-state mail-order nursery. He uses the nursery to locate varieties as distinctive as those found on the shelves of his vast library of botanical encyclopedias, such as a Mexican long-leafed pine he planted many years ago.

Among the many choice conifers in this homeowner-designed garden is a Mexican long-leafed pine.

Trips to the coast often produce interestingly shaped pieces of driftwood, which the owners add as accents to the dry stream and basin. An informal gravel path meanders through the shadiest part of the garden, where soft moss flourishes during the rainy season. But it is nature's rainbow of colors, appearing even more brilliant when surrounded by evergreens, that make this truly a garden for all seasons.

Stroll-style gardens are designed to be walked through and viewed from various points. The journey through this garden is marked by an unusual roof tile that features the face of a dragon.

Ten kara de mo
futtaru yōni
sakura kana.
—Issa (1763–1827)

[These cherry blossoms!
It's as if they fell
from heaven.]

Lush plantings and a bend in the path make the garden appear larger and lend a sense of mystery.

FROM GARDEN
TO HOUSE

From Frank Lloyd Wright to Sarah Susanka, some of America's most influential architects have been profoundly inspired by how traditional buildings in Japan harmonize with nature, rather than dominate it. Exterior space that blends easily with the house itself makes for a more satisfying living environment. Deriving inspiration from Japanese aesthetics, the entry spaces in this chapter welcome their inhabitants warmly and put visitors at ease.

At the behest of their then-ten-year-old daughter, David and Anne Montagna spent one Saturday afternoon casually browsing open houses when they stumbled upon a home that appealed to them immediately. So strongly did it resonate

A cascade of water flows under a bridge and continues alongside the brick path all the way to the front door.

This meandering waterfall is flanked by weeping conifers and evergreen shrubs. The concrete and brick path becomes a wooden bridge, which crosses the final threshold to the front door.

with the couple that they decided to make an offer on the spot, barely taking the time to inspect the home's interior. No one was more surprised than their daughter who had merely suggested what turned out to be a fateful family outing.

The special garden that leads up to the house presents a waterfall and stream that meander under and alongside a path of brick and wood. "We didn't have an affinity for Japanese aesthetics in particular, but we like nature and appreciate the use of wood and other natural materials, and after about two minutes we felt that this was meant to be our house," says David, who later went into the real estate business. Located in an area that has seen its share of palatial stucco mansions on treeless sites, the Montagnas' home looks as if it were meant to be there.

A Welcoming Entry in a Small Front Yard

Chadine Flood Gong created a welcoming entry for the owner of a modernist Eichler house. The distance between the sidewalk and the front door is small, with a slight curve in an existing brick path. To the right, in an area in front of the bedroom window, a stone water basin with recirculating water was placed. The overflow water runs into a concealed chamber below to be pumped back up the bamboo pipe. Traditionally, before entering the tea ceremony room, one

A low stone lantern, placed where light might be needed, guides visitors to the front door.

Doushitemo
ochiba fumaneba
yukenu michi.
—Suzuki Masajo (1906–2003)

No escaping it—
to take this path
I must walk on fallen
leaves.

washes one's hands and rinses one's mouth at the *chou-zubachi* (literally, hand water bowl), but here, the stone basin is placed for decoration. Surrounding plants are kept simple. Horsetail, a rush-like plant with bright green stems, grows profusely in a bed of baby's tears, and the existing brick pathway prevents its spread to unwanted areas. A stone lantern, ferns, and a Japanese maple complete the picture.

A low wooden fence separates the property of this home from the street.

LIVING WITH JAPANESE GARDENS

This beautiful residence epitomizes "living with Japanese gardens." It captures the controlled elegance and superlative craftsmanship that characterize modern homes built in the *sukiya* style. As Teiji Itoh and Yukio Futagawa noted in *The Elegant Japanese House*, this is the style "that Westerners generally mean when they speak of the beauty and elegance and uncluttered spaces of the Japanese house." Sukiya-style architecture is an ideal pursued by a select group of connoisseurs.

Richard Pascale, a writer, professor, and consultant, first became

Dusk falls upon a masterpiece of Japanese carpentry and its surrounding gardens.

Surrounding greenery sets off the fine lines of the timber-frame house.

aware of his affinity for Japanese aesthetics in the 1960s. A young engineer, he was in the U.S. Navy and was shipped to Japan, where he was stationed for two years. During this time, he developed a fascination with the Japanese culture and people. Upon returning to the United States, he had a desire to one day live in his own Japanese house and have his own Japanese garden.

In the 1970s, the success of Richard's first book, *The Art of Japanese Management*, afforded him the means to purchase a secluded house on one hundred and ten acres of land. When an earthquake destroyed the house, Richard then had an excuse to build the Japanese-style house and garden of his dreams. He hired architect Hiroshi Morimoto of Berkeley to design the house and Masaki Ueshima of Japan to design the garden. "Japanese philosophy, aesthetics, proportion, color, and texture are deeply rooted in my soul," says Morimoto, who has lived and studied extensively in both the United States and Japan. In particular, an emphasis on the relationship of interior areas to exterior surroundings informs his philosophy and is evident throughout what Richard calls "my sacred place."

Richard was personally involved with the installation of the garden, accompanying Ueshima to find just the right rocks from different areas of the country. Among the most stunning are rocks from Prescott, Arizona, that form the stone bridge over which one must cross to reach the home's front door.

As the house is actually two structures cleverly connected via an enclosed

The home's threshold is reached via a double-slab stone bridge that crosses a pond.

A stepping-stone path winds its way towards the home's more intimate quarters.

stairwell, the post-and-beam structure appears to be tucked into the garden rather than the other way around. The upper building, which houses the home's master bedroom suite and an office, can be accessed through a handsomely crafted gate and stepping-stone path. The design also takes advantage of a natural creek.

Richard made two observations after having the house and garden built—namely, that a house and garden ought to be designed with the garden in mind and that the developing and building of the garden should be done at the same time as the construction of the house. These two guidelines are necessary for the integration of the two and, in this case, to make it possible for cranes to place the large boulders.

"Coming here—it's instantly tonic!" exclaims Richard, whose forty-year love affair with Japanese aesthetics finds its true expression.

Building the house and gardens at the same time allowed for cranes to place large slabs and boulders, some weighing up to several tons each.

Above: Outside the bath, a small waterfall trickles gracefully.

Left: The closest thing to bathing alfresco: glass windows and walls wrap around the master bath.

Resources

Designers Whose Work Appears in this Book

Mark Bourne
Windsmith Design
San Carlos, CA
650.592.3590
www.windsmithdesign.com

Chadine Flood Gong
Chadine Interior Design/Chadine Japanese Garden Design
15910 Ravine Rd.
Los Gatos, CA 95030
408.354.0606
www.livingwithjapanesegardens.com

David Kato
Katoscapes
PO Box 2048
Los Gatos, CA 95031
408.353.2805
www.katoscapes.com

Hiro Morimoto
1200 Tenth St.
Berkeley, CA 94710
510.527.8800
www.morimotoarch.com

LISA PARRAMORE
522 Vincent Dr.
Mountain View, CA 94041
650.966.8238
www.livingwithjapanesegardens.com

TOP 10 PUBLIC JAPANESE GARDENS IN NORTH AMERICA*

*Results of the *Journal of Japanese Gardening's* 2004 Public Garden Survey

ANDERSON JAPANESE GARDENS
318 Spring Creek Rd.
Rockford, IL 61107
815.229.9390
www.andersongardens.org

THE BLOEDEL RESERVE
7571 NE Dolphin Dr.
Bainbridge Island, WA 98110
206.842.7631
www.bloedelreserve.org

THE JAPANESE GARDEN AT THE
DONALD C. TILLMAN WATER RECLAMATION PLANT
6100 Woodley Ave.
Van Nuys, CA 91406
818.756.8166
www.lacity.org/san/japanesegarden

JAPANESE-AMERICAN CULTURAL AND COMMUNITY CENTER
244 S. San Pedro St.
Los Angeles, CA 90012
213.628.2725
www.jaccc.org

JŌ JYŌ EN
(The Garden of Quiet Listening)
Carleton College
104 Maple St.
Northfield, MN 55057

THE MORIKAMI MUSEUM AND JAPANESE GARDENS
4000 Morikami Park Rd.
Delray Beach, FL 33446
561.495.0233
www.morikami.org

NITOBE MEMORIAL GARDEN UBC
6501 NW Marine Dr.
Vancouver, British Columbia V6T 1Z4
Canada
604.822.9666
www.ubcbotanicalgarden.org/nitobe

PORTLAND JAPANESE GARDEN
Washington Park
611 SW Kingston Ave.
Portland, OR 97201
503.223.1321
www.japanesegarden.com

SEATTLE JAPANESE GARDEN
Washington Park Arboretum
Lake Washington Blvd. East (north of East Madison St.)
Seattle, WA 98112
206.684.4725
www.seattle.gov/parks/parkspaces/gardens.htm

SHOFUSO JAPANESE HOUSE AND GARDEN
Horticultural Center, West Fairmount Park
North Horticultural Dr.
Philadelphia, PA 19131
215.878.5097

ADDITIONAL RESOURCES

BAMBOO GIANT NURSERY
(bamboo plants and products)
5601 Freedom Blvd.
Aptos, CA 95003
831.687.0100
www.bamboogiant.com

BAMBOO SOURCERY
(bamboo plants and books about bamboo, fences, and garden accessories)
666 Wagnon Rd.
Sebastopol, CA 95472
707.823.5866
www.bamboosourcery.com

THE JAPANESE GARDEN DATABASE
(comprehensive directory of Japanese gardens, designers, resources)
www.jgarden.org

JAPANESE GIFTS
(common garden fences and ornaments for the Japanese garden)
www.japanesegifts.com

JOURNAL OF JAPANESE GARDENING
ROTH TEI-EN
(a bimonthly publication dedicated to Japanese gardening and architecture)
PO Box 1050
Rockport, ME 04856
207.273.2907
www.rothteien.com

PORTERHOWSE FARMS AND ARBORETUM
(a nursery, including mail order, with a large selection of conifers)
41370 SE Thomas Rd.
Sandy, OR 97055
503.668.5834
www.porterhowse.com

STONE FOREST
(hand-carved granite artifacts and sculptures)
213 S. St. Francis Dr.
Santa Fe, NM 87501
888.682.2987
www.stoneforest.com

PHOTO CREDITS

Gong, Chadine Flood, 50
Livingston, David, 3, 4
Parramore, Lisa, 58, 59, 60
Rice, Ken, 35 (top)
Turnage, Anna, 10, 84